W9-DID-505

PRESENTED   TO

_____

B Y

_____

D A T E

_____

SUCCESS

ONE DAY AT A TIME

JOHN C. MAXWELL

J . COUNTRYMAN
NASHVILLE, TENNESSEE

ACKNOWLEDGEMENTS

Grateful acknowledgement is made to Thomas Nelson Publishers
for permission to reprint from the following books.

Maxwell, John C. 2000. *Failing Forward:*
Turning Mistakes into Stepping Stones for Success.
Nashville, Tennessee: Thomas Nelson Publishers.

Maxwell, John C. 1999. *The 21 Indispensable Qualities of a Leader:*
Becoming the Person Others Will Want to Follow. Nashville, Tennessee:
Thomas Nelson Publishers.

Maxwell, John C. 1997. *The Success Journey: The Process of Living*
Your Dreams. Nashville, Tennessee: Thomas Nelson Publishers.

Copyright © 2000 by Maxwell Motivation, Inc., Norcross, Georgia 30092

Published by J. Countryman®, a division of Thomas Nelson, Inc.,
Nashville, Tennessee 37214

All rights reserved. No portion of this publication may be reproduced, stored in a
retrieval system, or transmitted in any form by any means—electronic, mechanical,
photocopying, recording, or any other—except for brief quotations in printed
reviews, without the prior written permission of the publisher.

J. Countryman® is a trademark of Thomas Nelson Inc.

Project editor—Jenny Baumgartner

Designed by David Uttley Design, Sisters, Oregon

ISBN 0-8499-5511-4

Published in association with Sealy M. Yates, Literary Agent, Orange, California

Printed and bound in Belgium

www.jcountryman.com

You will never change your life

until you change something you do daily.

The secret of your success is found

in your daily routine.

— J O H N   C .   M A X W E L L

W ho *doesn't* desire success? It may seem peculiar to ask that question. Yet most of the people you know will never achieve success. They'll dream about it. They'll talk about it. But most of them won't possess it. And that's a shame.

Why is that? Because most people don't understand success. It isn't the lottery. You don't stop at the corner convenience store on the way home, buy a ticket, and then wait for success to strike. Nor is it a place you find when you reach some magical time of life. Success is not a destination thing—it's a daily thing. The only way to achieve real success is to do it *one day at a time.*

THE TRUTH ABOUT SUCCESS

To be successful, you don't need to be lucky or rich. But you do need to know this:

- You are what you do daily.
- You first form your habits; then your habits form you.
- It is just as easy to form habits of success as it is to form habits of failure.

Every day you live, you are in the process of becoming. Whether you are becoming better or worse depends on what you give yourself to. Please allow me to give you some advice on how to make yourself successful.

SEVEN STEPS TO SUCCESS

1. Make a commitment to grow daily. One of the greatest mistakes people make is that they have the wrong focus. Success doesn't come from acquiring, achieving, or advancing. It comes only as the result of growing. If you make it your goal to grow a little every day, it won't be long before you begin to see positive results in your life. As the poet Robert Browning said, "Why stay on earth except to grow?"

2. Value the process more than events. Specific life events are good for making decisions, but it's the process of change and growth that has lasting value. If you want to go to the next level, strive for continual improvement.

3. Don't wait for inspiration. Basketball great Jerry West said, "You can't get much done in life if you only work on the days when you feel good." The people who go far do so because they motivate themselves and give life their best, regardless of how they feel. To be successful, persevere.

4. Be willing to sacrifice pleasure for opportunity. One of the greatest lessons my father taught me was the principle of *pay now; play later.* For everything in life, you pay a price. You choose whether you will pay it on the front end or the back end. If you pay first, then you will enjoy greater rewards in the end—and those rewards taste sweeter.

5. Dream big. It doesn't pay to dream small. Robert J. Kriegel and Louis Patler, authors of *If It Ain't Broke, Break It*, assert, "We don't have a clue as to what people's limits are. All the tests, stopwatches, and finish lines in the world can't measure human potential. When someone is pursuing their dream, they'll go far beyond what seems to be their limitations. The potential that exists within us is limitless and largely untapped. When you think of limits, you create them."

6. Plan your priorities. One thing that all successful people have in common is that they have mastered the ability to manage their time. First and foremost, they have organized themselves. Henry Kaiser, founder of Kaiser Aluminum and Kaiser Permanente Health Care, says, "Every minute spent in planning will save you two in execution." You never regain lost time, so make the most of every moment.

7. Give up to go up. Nothing of value comes without sacrifice. Life is filled with critical moments when you will have the opportunity to trade one thing you value for another. Keep your eyes open for such moments—and always be sure to trade up, not down.

If you dedicate yourself to these seven steps, then you will keep improving—and you will be successful. Your growth may not be obvious to others all at once, but *you* will see your progress almost immediately. And though recognition from others may come slowly, don't lose heart. Keep working at it. You will succeed in the end.

As you progress on this daily journey, use this book to jump-start your attitude and your insights. Read through the whole thing in a sitting or two. Then put it on your nightstand, in your car, or in your briefcase. When you have a moment, flip through its pages to remind you of what it means to achieve success.

It's going to be an incredible journey! Sometimes you will experience excitement; other times, only discipline will carry you through. But always remember: Success is waiting for you to make the first move. Let's get started.

JOHN C. MAXWELL

SPRING 2000

THE KEY TO SUCCESS

Many people who came before you searched for success and never found it. They thought of it as the Holy Grail or the Fountain of Youth—something to be captured at the end of a long quest. Some believed it was a relationship to be won. Others supposed it was a position to be earned or an object to be possessed.

But success is none of those things. It's not a destination to be reached. It is a process—a journey to be taken. And you do it one day at a time.

It takes most people some time to discover what God created them for. If you are willing, you can explore the world and learn more about your purpose every day. You can engage in activities that help you grow a little more in mind, body, or spirit. And you can perform some act—large or small—that helps others.

Success is knowing your purpose in life, sowing seeds that benefit others, and growing to your maximum potential.

The door to your potential is waiting for you. The key is to be on the journey. Keep at it day in and day out. If you are, you're a success today. And you'll be a success tomorrow.

DREAM

[EVERY DAY]

Behind me is infinite power.
Before me is endless possibility.
Around me is boundless opportunity.
Why should I fear?

— STELLA STUART

NURTURE
YOUR "CHILDREN"

Do you take care of your "children"? You may never have thought of your dreams as children, but that's what they are. They are your offspring—the joy of your today and the hope of your future. Protect them. Feed them. Nurture them. Encourage them to grow. Care for them. For someday, they may take care of you.

Cherish your visions

and your dreams as they are the

children of your soul;

the blueprints of your ultimate

achievements.

— NAPOLEON HILL

NEEDED: PEOPLE!

You cannot do it on your own. You will need the help of others—and you will need to give help to others—if you want to be successful. And that will require you to connect with others. To do that, follow these suggestions:

- Focus on people.
- Be likable.
- Show others that you care.
- Remember everyone's name.
- Walk slowly through the crowd.
- Be generous.

SEVEN SECRETS OF SUCCESS

There is no secret of success.
Success is for everyone.

Your life becomes better only when
you become better.

There is no success without sacrifice.

Success is achieved in inches,
not miles.

The greatest enemy of tomorrow's success
is today's success.

No advice on success works unless you do.

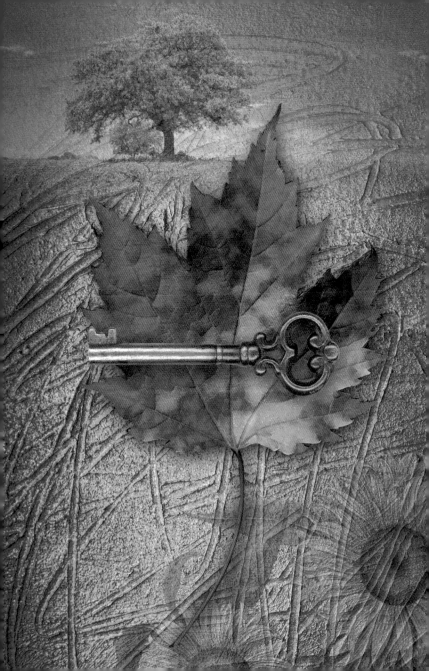

LESSON FROM A FARMER

 A young man from the city graduated from college with a degree in journalism and got a job at a small-town newspaper. One of his first assignments was to interview an old farmer who lived twenty miles outside of town. As he sat with the grizzled man on his front porch, the young journalist looked at his notepad and started asking his questions. One of the first he asked was, "Sir, what time do you go to work in the morning?"

The old farmer chuckled and replied, "Son, I don't *go* to work. I'm surrounded by it."

We can learn a lesson from the old farmer. Opportunities are a lot like his work. They are everywhere. But the problem is that we often don't have the eyes to see them.

As you approach each day, look around. Be aware. If you don't see opportunities, remember that it's not because they aren't there. You're *always* surrounded by them. You simply need to open your eyes and see them. Then act on them.

WANTED!

More to *improve and* fewer to *disapprove.*

More *doers* and fewer *talkers.*

More to say *it can be done*
and fewer to say *it's impossible.*

More to *inspire* others
and fewer to *throw cold water* on them.

More to *get into the thick of things*
and fewer to *sit on the sidelines.*

More to point out *what's right*
and fewer to *show what's wrong.*

More to *light a candle*
and fewer to *curse the darkness.*

— AUTHOR UNKNOWN

You will be as

small as your controlling desire,

as great as your dominant

aspiration.

—JAMES ALLEN

FIND YOUR VISION

O ne of the great dreamers of the twentieth century was Walt Disney. Any person who could create the first sound cartoon, first all-color cartoon, and first animated feature-length motion picture is definitely someone with vision. But Disney's greatest masterpieces of vision were Disneyland and Walt Disney World. And the spark for that vision came from an unexpected place.

Back when Walt's two daughters were young, he used to take them to an amusement park in the Los Angeles area on Saturday mornings. His girls loved it, and he did too. Amusement parks are a kid's paradise, with wonderful atmosphere: the smell of popcorn and cotton candy, the gaudy colors of signs advertising rides, and the sound of kids screaming as the roller coaster plummets over a hill.

Walt was especially captivated by the carousel. As he approached it, he saw a blur of bright images racing around to the tune of energetic calliope music. But when he got closer and the carousel stopped, he could see that his eye had been fooled. He observed shabby horses with cracked and chipped paint. And he noticed that only the horses on the outside row moved up and down. The others stood lifeless, bolted to the floor.

The cartoonist's disappointment inspired him with a grand vision. In his mind's eye he could see an amusement park where the illusion didn't evaporate, where children and adults could enjoy a carnival atmosphere without the seedy side that accompanies some circuses or traveling carnivals. His dream became Disneyland. As Larry Taylor stated in *Be an Orange*, Walt's vision could be summarized as, "No chipped paint. All the horses jump."

. . . For Disney, vision was never a problem. Because of his creativity and desire for excellence, he always saw what *could* be. If you lack vision, look inside yourself. Draw on your natural gifts and desires. Look to your calling if you have one. And if you still don't sense a vision of your own, then consider hooking up with a leader whose vision resonates with you.

FROM *The 21 Indispensable Qualities of a Leader*

ONE STEP FURTHER

Do more than exist: live.

Do more than touch: feel.

Do more than look: observe.

Do more than read: absorb.

Do more than hear: listen.

Do more than listen: understand.

Do more than think: reflect.

Do more than just talk: say something.

— AUTHOR UNKNOWN

MRS. FIELD'S
RECIPE FOR SUCCESS

Love what you're doing.

Believe in your product.

Select good people.

— DEBBI FIELDS

*People who have given up are
ruled by their darkest mistakes, worst failures,
and deepest regrets. If you want to be successful,
then be governed by your finest thoughts,
your highest enthusiasm, your greatest optimism,
and your most triumphant experiences.*

— JOHN C. MAXWELL

It's Easier

It's easier to settle for average
than strive for achievement.

It's easier to be saturated with complacency
than stirred with compassion.

It's easier to be skeptical
than successful.

It's easier to question
than conquer.

It's easier to rationalize your disappointments
than realize your dreams.

It's easier to belch the baloney
than bring home the bacon.

— AUTHOR UNKNOWN

Opportunities and motivation are connected. Motivated people see opportunities, and opportunities are often what motivate people.

Great attitudes precede great opportunities. Who you are determines what you see.

Today is the best day for an opportunity. Opportunity always takes "now" for an answer.

Opportunities are the result of pluck, not luck. The people who succeed seek out opportunities, and if they can't find them, they create them.

Opportunities don't present themselves in ideal circumstances. If you wait for all the lights to turn green, you will never leave your driveway.

Opportunity without commitment will be lost. Abandoned opportunities are never lost—they are simply pursued by the competition.

Opportunity is birthed out of problems. If you're looking for a BIG opportunity, find a BIG problem.

Opportunities either multiply or disappear. The more opportunities you pursue, the more you find behind them.

Opportunities must be nourished if they are to survive. As Peter Drucker, the father of modern management, says, "Feed an opportunity; starve a problem."

To do a common thing uncommonly

well brings success.

— HENRY JOHN HEINZ

To laugh often and much;

To win the respect of intelligent people

and the affection of children,

to earn the appreciation of honest critics

and endure the betrayal of false friends;

to appreciate beauty, to find the best in others,

to leave the world a bit better

whether by a healthy child, a garden patch,

or a redeemed social condition;

to know even one life has breathed easier

because you lived.

This is to have succeeded.

— RALPH WALDO EMERSON

I was a guy who practiced until the blisters bled, and then practiced some more. When I was a kid I carried my bat to class with me. I'd run a buddy's newspaper route if I could get him to shag flies for me. When I played for San Diego, I paid kids to shag flies on my days off.

— TED WILLIAMS,
GREATEST BASEBALL HITTER
OF ALL TIME

Think "tomorrow."

Make today's efforts pay off tomorrow.

Free the imagination.

You are capable of more than you can imagine—

so imagine the ultimate.

Strive for lasting quality.

"Good enough" never is.

Have "stick-to-it-ivity."

Never, never, *never* give up.

Have fun.

You're never truly a success until you

enjoy what you are doing.

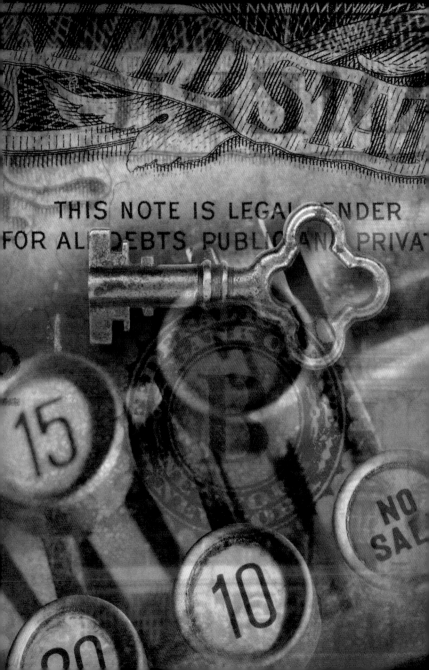

JUST WHAT THE DOCTOR ORDERED

 A young entrepreneur in Gilmer, Texas, opened a fast-food franchise along with two partners. During their first week in operation, he overheard two little old ladies in the restaurant talking about their disappointment with the soft drink selection. One of the ladies, who was diabetic, wished they had Diet Dr. Pepper.

The entrepreneur got in his car, drove to the nearest convenience store, purchased a six-pack of Diet Dr. Pepper, and returned to his restaurant. Then he brought the lady a cup of ice and a can of the drink.

"Ma'am," he said, "There will always be a case of Diet Dr. Pepper with your name on it in a refrigerator in the back. Anytime you come in, you just tell the person at the counter who you are and that you would like a Diet Dr. Pepper, and they'll get it for you."

The woman was shocked.

"Young man," she said, "I have lived in this town my whole life. I have many influential friends, and they will all hear what you just did for me. Thank you. From now on, we will be regular customers." And she was as good as her word.

THE GREATEST GENERAL

A man died and met Saint Peter

at the gates of heaven. Recognizing the saint's

knowledge and wisdom, he wanted to ask him a question.

"Saint Peter," he said, "I have been interested in military

history for many years. Tell me, who was

the greatest general of all times?"

Peter quickly responded, "O, that is a simple question.

It's that man right over there."

The man looked where Peter was pointing and answered,

"You must be mistaken. I knew that man on earth,

and he was just a common laborer."

"That's right," Peter remarked,

"but he would have been the greatest general

of all time — if he had been a general."

— MARK TWAIN

All You Can

Do all the good you can,

By all the means you can,

In all the ways you can,

In all the places you can,

At all the times you can,

To all the people you can,

As long as ever you can.

— JOHN WESLEY

It is your duty to find yourself.

— JOHN C. MAXWELL

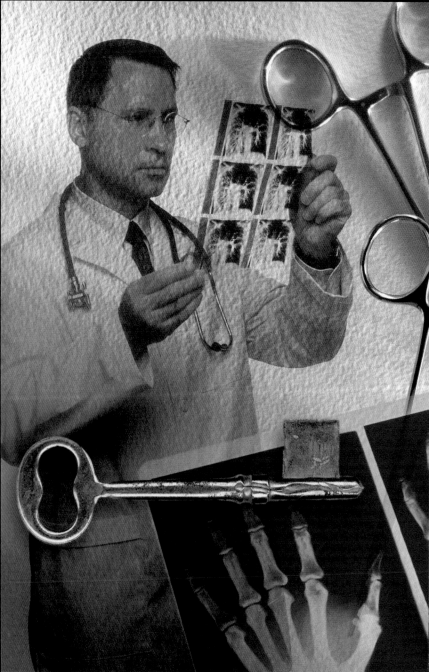

IT'S NEVER TOO LATE

Robert Lopatin thought it was too late. As a boy, he had dreamed of becoming a doctor. But when he went to college, he gave up the idea. Instead, he went into the family business of manufacturing women's clothing. He stayed there for twenty-seven years! Then he and his father sold their business. If he wished, he could retire.

But then, at a friend's wedding, he sat next to a young man who had just finished medical school. Chatting with the new doctor made him think about his boyhood dream. And at age fifty-one, Robert Lopatin decided to become a doctor.

Today he is fifty-five. He graduated from the Albert Einstein College of Medicine and is currently serving his residency at Montefiore Medical Center in Bronx, New York. And he's loving it—even the one-hundred hour workweeks and the graveyard shifts.

"I feel like I died and was born again," he says.

You may have a dream in your heart that you think is too old to pursue. Another person may have told you that it's too late to do what you desire. But it's not. Writer Joseph Conrad published his first novel at age forty. Robert Lopatin will be in his late fifties when he begins to practice medicine as a full-fledged doctor. Artist Grandma Moses started painting when she was seventy-five years old—and she still had a twenty-six-year career. Pursue your dream, no matter how farfetched it may seem.

EXERCISE FOR SUCCESS

Think of the pursuit of your dream as being like a major athletic event. Train for it. As you prepare and "exercise," you will get stronger—mentally, emotionally, and physically. To successfully achieve your dream, you need to keep improving. The best way to do that is to . . .

- Keep your body fit.
- Keep your heart flexible.
- Keep your mind open.
- Keep your comfort zone expanding.

Everybody can be great . . .

because anybody can serve. You don't have to

have a college degree to serve.

You don't have to make your subject and verb

agree to serve. You only need a heart full of grace.

A soul generated by love.

— MARTIN LUTHER KING JR.

All the beautiful

sentiments in the world weigh less

than a single lovely action.

— JAMES RUSSELL LOWELL

He who is afraid

of doing too much always

does too little.

— GERMAN PROVERB

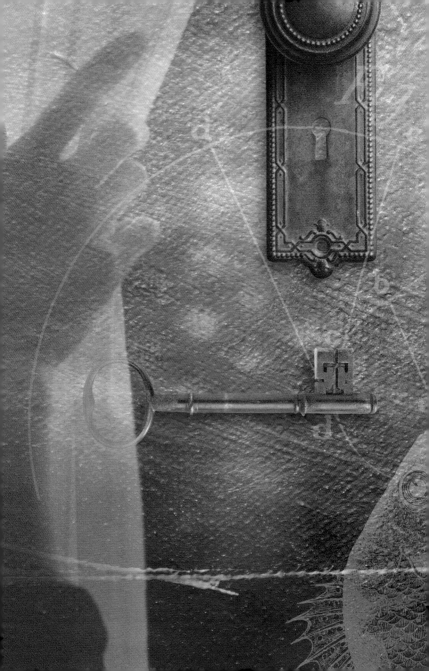

PERSEVERE

[EVERY DAY]

Never give up then,
for that is just the place and time
that the tide will turn.

— HARRIET BEECHER STOW

DO YOURSELF A FAVOR

A poor, hungry young man sat moping on a bridge, watching a group of fishermen. Looking into a basket and seeing a bunch of fish nearby, the young man said, "Boy, if I had a mess of fish like that, I'd be in good shape. I'd sell them and buy some clothes and something to eat."

"I'll give you that many fish if you do a small favor for me," a fisherman replied.

"Sure."

"Tend this line for me awhile. I've got some errands to do up the street," said the older man.

The young man gladly accepted the offer. As he tended the man's pole, the fish were really biting, and he reeled in one fish after another. It wasn't long before he was smiling, enjoying the activity.

When the older man returned, he said, "I want to give you the fish I promised. Here, take all the fish you caught. But I also want to give you a piece of advice. The next time you're in need, don't waste time daydreaming and wishing for what could be. Get busy, cast the line yourself, and make something happen."

A THORN IN YOUR SIDE?

As you discover your purpose in life and pursue your dreams, you will inevitably spend more and more of your time doing what you enjoy and do best. That's good. You can achieve your dreams only if you focus on your priorities.

But success requires something else: discipline. One of the best ways I know to improve discipline is to do something you don't enjoy doing—every day. If you learn to do what you must, you will be able to do what you want.

Do something you hate every day,

just for the practice.

— J O H N C. M A X W E L L

Success seems to

be connected with action.

Successful people keep moving.

They make mistakes,

but they don't quit.

— CONRAD HILTON

*Success is going from
failure to failure without losing
your enthusiasm.*

— A B R A H A M   L I N C O L N

*If you keep doing
what you've always done,
you'll always get what you've
always gotten.*

— J O H N   C .   M A X W E L L

TALENT IS OVERRATED

Dr. Benjamin Bloom of the University of Chicago conducted a five-year study of leading artists, athletes, and scholars. It consisted of anonymous interviews with the top twenty performers in various fields, including pianists, Olympic swimmers, tennis players, sculptors, mathematicians, and neurologists. That information was supplemented by additional interviews with those people's families and teachers. Bloom and his team of researchers sought to find clues to how these high achievers developed. What they discovered was that drive and determination—not talent—led to their success.

NO SHORTCUTS

William Danforth, who became the owner of the huge Ralston Purina Company, learned a lesson about success when he was a young man. He said, "When I was sixteen, I came to St. Louis to attend the Manual Training School. It was a mile from my boardinghouse to the school. A teacher, who lived nearby, and I would start for school at the same time every morning. But he always beat me there. Even back then I didn't want to be beaten, and so I tried all the shortcuts. Day after day, however, he arrived ahead of me. Then I discovered how he did it. When he came to each street crossing, he would run to the other curb. The thing that put him ahead of me was just 'that little extra.'"

There are no shortcuts

to any place worth going.

— BEVERLY SILLS

Failure is really a matter of conceit.

People don't work hard because,

in their conceit, they imagine they'll succeed

without ever making an effort.

Most people believe that they'll

wake up some day and find themselves rich.

Actually, they've got it half right,

because eventually they do wake up.

— THOMAS EDISON

LONG ON IDEAS

Life magazine named him the number one man of the millennium. The number of things he invented is astounding—1,093. He held more patents than any other person in the world, having been granted at least one patent every year for sixty-five consecutive years. His name was Thomas Edison.

Most people credit Edison's ability to creative genius. He credited it to hard work. "Genius," he declared, "is ninety-nine percent perspiration and one percent inspiration." I believe his success was also the result of a third factor: his positive attitude.

Edison was an optimist who saw the best in everything. "If we did all the things we were capable of doing," he once said, "we would literally astound ourselves." When it took him ten thousand tries to find the right materials for the incandescent light bulb, he didn't see them as that many failures. With each attempt he gained information about what didn't work, bringing him closer to a solution. He never doubted that he would find a good one. His belief could be summarized by his statement: "Many of life's failures are people who did not realize how close they were to success when they gave up."

Probably the most notable display of Edison's positive attitude can be seen in the way he approached a tragedy that occurred when he was in his late sixties. The lab he had built in West Orange, New Jersey, was world famous. He called the fourteen-building complex his invention factory. Its main building was massive—greater than three football fields in size. From that base of operations, he and his staff conceived of inventions, developed prototypes, manufactured products, and shipped them to customers. It became a model for modern research and manufacturing.

Edison loved the place. . . . But on a December day in 1914, his beloved lab caught fire. As he stood outside and watched it burn, he is reported to have said, "Kids, go get your mother. She'll never see another fire like this one."

Most people would have been crushed. Not Edison. "I am sixty-seven," he said after the tragedy, "but not too old to make a fresh start. I've been through a lot of things like this." He rebuilt the lab, and he kept working for another seventeen years. "I am long on ideas, but short on time," he commented. "I expect to live to be only about a hundred." He died at age eighty-four.

If Edison hadn't been such a positive person, he never

would have achieved such success as an inventor. If you look at the lives of people in any profession who achieve lasting success, you will find that they almost always possess a positive outlook on life.

FROM *THE 21 INDISPENSABLE QUALITIES OF A LEADER*

There is no defeat

except in no longer trying. There is no

defeat save within,

no really insurmountable barrier,

save our own inherent weakness

of purpose.

— ELBERT HUBBARD

THE SIX PHASES OF
A PROJECT

PHASE ONE:

ENTHUSIASM

PHASE TWO:

DISILLUSIONMENT

PHASE THREE:

PANIC

PHASE FOUR:

THE SEARCH FOR THE GUILTY

PHASE FIVE:

PUNISHMENT OF THE INNOCENT

PHASE SIX:

PRAISE AND HONOR
FOR THE NONPARTICIPANTS

— SOURCE UNKNOWN

Success is not measured

by what a man accomplishes,

but by the opposition he has encountered,

and the courage with which he

has maintained the struggle against

overwhelming odds.

— C H A R L E S L I N D B E R G H

THE WAY TO THE TOP

My friend Zig Ziglar once told me that he visited the Washington Monument on a trip to Washington, D.C. As he arrived with some friends, he heard a guide announce, "Ladies and gentlemen, there is currently a two-hour wait to ride the elevator to the top of the monument." The guide then paused a moment, smiled, and added, "However, there is *no wait* should you desire to take the stairs."

Zig's story reveals something about success. In truth, there are no elevators to the top. If you want to make it there, you've got to take a long series of steps. How many steps you're willing to take—and how long you're willing to keep climbing—determines how high you will go.

I am a great believer in luck,

and I find that the harder I work,

the more I have of it.

— STEPHEN LEACOCK

G E N I U S !

Sarasate, the greatest

Spanish violinist of the nineteenth century,

was once called a genius by a famous critic.

In reply to this, Sarasate declared,

"Genius! For thirty-seven years

I've practiced fourteen hours a day, and now

they call me a genius."

— J O H N   C .   M A X W E L L

You can become the star of the hour if you

make the minutes count.

— A N O N Y M O U S

Every worthwhile accomplishment

has a price tag attached to it.

The question is always whether you are

willing to pay the price to attain it—

in hard work, sacrifice, patience,

faith, and endurance.

— JOHN C. MAXWELL

A year from now you

may wish you had started today.

— KAREN LAMB

Napoleon wrote that the reason why he beat the Austrians was that they did not know the value of five minutes. It took Lincoln less than five minutes to deliver his immortal Gettysburg Address. It took William Jennings Bryan less than five minutes to electrify a great political convention with but a single expression that gave him the nomination for the presidency of the United States.

— GEORGE MATTHEW ADAMS

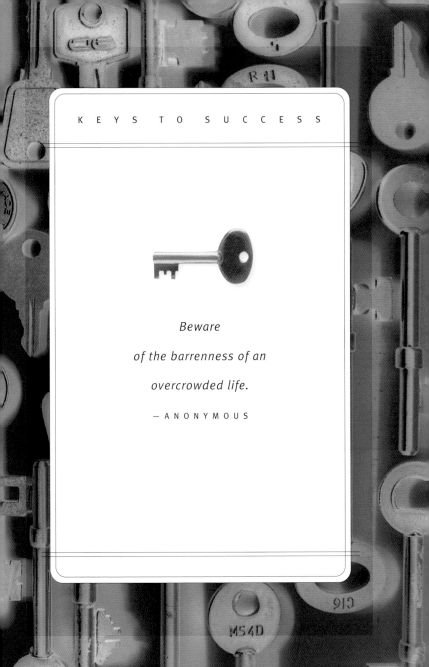

KEYS TO SUCCESS

Beware

of the barrenness of an

overcrowded life.

— ANONYMOUS

By perseverance

the snail reached the ark.

— CHARLES SPURGEON

―――――――

Success is a little like wrestling a gorilla.

You don't quit when you're tired —

you quit when the gorilla is tired.

— ROBERT STRAUSS

―――――――

It takes twenty years

to make an overnight success.

— EDDIE CANTOR

THEY CALLED IT LUCK

He worked by day
and toiled by night.

He gave up play
and much delight.

Dry books he read,
new things to learn.

And forged ahead,
success to earn.

He plodded on,
with faith and pluck.

And when he won,
they called it luck.

— AUTHOR UNKNOWN

WIN THE DAILY BATTLE

People who achieve daily success have learned
to conquer four common time-wasters.

Laziness:
Time put to no useful purpose,
not even relaxation.

Procrastination:
Putting off things that should be done now.

Distraction:
Time frittered away on the details of side issues,
to the detriment of the main issue.

Impatience:
Lack of preparation, thoroughness,
or perseverance, usually resulting in
time-consuming mistakes.

Do It Today

Do the right thing;

Do it today;

Do it with no hope of return or promise of reward;

Do it with a smile and a cheerful attitude;

Do it day after day after day.

Do it, and someday,

There will come a day

That will be a payday

For all the yesterdays

You spent focused on the current day—

That will not only give value to today,

But will make each future day

Outshine each yesterday.

And what more could you ask of a day?

A MOST VALUABLE LESSON

John Erskine learned the most valuable lesson of his life when he was only fourteen years old. His piano teacher asked him, "How many times a week do you practice, and how long do you practice each time?"

He told her that he tried to practice once daily for an hour or more.

"Don't do that," she responded. "When you grow up, time won't come in long stretches. Practice in minutes, whenever you can find them—five or ten before school, after lunch, between chores. Spread your practice throughout the day, and music will become a part of your life."

Her advice obviously worked. Erskine became a concert pianist who performed with the New York Philharmonic, and he later served as president of the Juilliard School of Music and director of the Metropolitan Opera Association. He also went on to teach literature at Columbia University and wrote more than forty-five books. His most famous work, *The Private Life of Helen of Troy*, was written as he commuted to Columbia.

The Eight "P" Plan for Achievement

Plan Purposefully.

Prepare Prayerfully.

Proceed Positively.

Pursue Persistently.

— AUTHOR UNKNOWN

Success is 99 percent failure.

— SOICHIRO HONDA

It's so simple that it's revolutionary. The fact is, this formula or principle is misunderstood enough, or overlooked enough, that it can truly be called magic by those who understand it. Ready? Here it is. You beat 50 percent of the people in America by working hard. You beat another 40 percent by being a person of honesty and integrity and standing for something.

The last 10 percent is a dogfight in the free enterprise system.

— ART WILLIAMS

A success is one who decided to succeed —
and worked.

A failure is one who decided to succeed —
and wished.

A decided failure is one who failed to decide —
and waited.

— WILLIAM A. WARD

Far better it is to dare mighty things,

to win glorious triumphs,

even though checkered with failure,

than to take rank with those poor spirits who

neither enjoy much nor suffer much because

they live in the gray twilight that knows not

victory nor defeat.

— THEODORE ROOSEVELT

How Do You
Spell Success?

Select your goal.

Unlock your personal potential.

Commit yourself to your plan.

Chart your course.

Expect problems.

Stand firm on your commitment.

Surrender everything to God.

GRØW

[EVERY DAY]

Stop what you're doing long

enough to grow.

— J O H N   C .   M A X W E L L

Success is never final.

— WINSTON CHURCHILL

No one has ever

made a significant impact after

they won the Nobel Prize.

— PETER DRUCKER

CHANGE THE WORLD

The following words are inscribed on the tomb of an Anglican bishop in Westminster Abby (1100 A.D.).

When I was young and free and my imagination had no limits, I dreamed of changing the world. As I grew older and wiser, I discovered the world would not change, so I shortened my sights somewhat and decided to change only my country.

But it, too, seemed immovable.

As I grew into my twilight years, in one last desperate attempt, I settled for changing only my family, those closest to me, but alas, they would have none of it.

And now as I lie on my deathbed, I suddenly realize: If I had only changed myself first, then my example I would have changed my family.

From their inspiration and encouragement, I would then have been able to better my country, and, who knows, I may have even changed the world.

WHICH WAY ARE YOU DRIVING?

People always have two conflicting bents when it comes to their work:

The first is the drive *to have*. It pushes people to focus on what they can *get* out of their jobs—a higher salary, a bigger office, greater status, a better position.

The second is the desire *to be*. It prompts people to think about what they can *give* to their organizations—their very best to ensure that everyone succeeds.

FORMULA FOR SUCCESS

Instruction + Example x Experience = Success

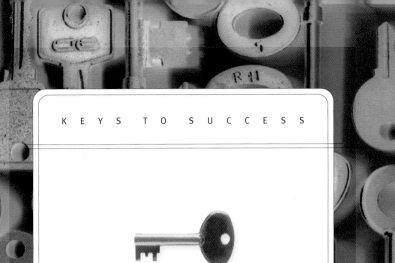

K E Y S   T O   S U C C E S S

Without rest,

a man cannot work.

Without work,

the rest does not give

you any benefit.

— A B K H A S I A N   P R O V E R B

REAL SUCCESS

I believe that to succeed, a person needs only four things. You can remember them by thinking of the word REAL.

Relationships: The greatest skill needed for success is the ability to get along with other people. It impacts every aspect of a person's life. Your relationships make you or break you.

Equipping: One of the greatest lessons I've learned in life is that those closest to you determine the level of your success. If your dreams are great, you achieve them only with a team.

Attitude: People's attitudes determine how they approach life day-to-day. Your attitude, more than your aptitude, will determine your altitude.

Leadership: Everything rises and falls on leadership. If you desire to "lift the lid" on your personal effectiveness, the only way to do it is to increase your leadership skills.

If you dedicate yourself to growing in these four areas, then it doesn't matter what kind of work you do. You will become successful.

FROM *FAILING FORWARD*

Success is waking up

in the morning, whoever you are,

wherever you are,

however old or young,

and bounding out of bed because

there's something out there that

you love to do, that you believe in,

that you're good at—

something that's bigger than you are,

and you can hardly wait to

get at it again today.

— WHIT HOBBS

1. **Trade the first half for the second half.** Much of the first half of life is spent paying the price for later success. The greater dues you pay now, the more they compound, and the greater potential for a successful second half.

2. **Trade affirmation for accomplishment.** Accolades fade quickly, but your accomplishments have the potential to make a positive impact on the lives of others.

3. **Trade financial gain for future potential.** The temptation is almost always to go for the "big bucks." But seeking to have greater potential almost always leads to a higher return— including financially.

4. **Trade immediate pleasure for personal growth.** It takes an oak tree decades to grow, but it takes a squash only weeks. Which do you want to be?

5. **Trade exploration for focus.** The younger you are, the more experimenting you should do. But once you've found what you were created to do, stick with it.

6.   **Trade quantity of life for quality of life.** Your life is not a dress rehearsal. Give it your best because you won't get another chance.

7.   **Trade security for significance.** The great men and women of history were great not because of what they owned or earned, but because they gave their lives to accomplish greatness.

8.   **Trade acceptable for excellence.** If something is worth doing, either give it your best or don't do it at all.

9.   **Trade addition for multiplication.** When you invest in others, you multiply your efforts—every person you assist becomes a fellow workmate.

10. **Trade your work for God for a walk with God.** No matter how much you value your work, it cannot compare with a relationship with your Creator.

You have reached

the pinnacle of success as soon as

you become uninterested in money,

compliments, or publicity.

— O .   A .   B A T T I S T A

A GIFT LEFT IN THE CASE

Niccolò Paganini is considered one of the greatest violinists of all time. He was a virtuoso, performing his first concert at age eleven. His great technical ability revolutionized violin technique across Europe.

When he died in 1840, he willed his violin to Genoa, Italy, the place of his birth. But he did so upon one condition: that no other artist ever play his instrument again. Glad to have the violin come into their possession, the city's fathers agreed to the request, and they put it in a beautiful case for everyone to see.

But wooden instruments have a certain peculiarity. As long as they are handled, they show no wear. But if one lay unused, it begins to decay, which is what happened to Paganini's violin. His once-exquisite instrument became worm-eaten and useless. Other violins of the same vintage have been handed down through the generations, from one gifted musician to another, and they continue to bring great music to attentive audiences. But Paganini's violin is a crumbling relic of what it once was.

The talent you have been given by God cannot be set aside like Paganini's violin. If you do not nurture your ability, it will steadily decay until it is useless. But if you consistently work with it, diligently trying to bring out its best, it will bring forth "music" that will not only give you joy, but will also serve others and bring you success.

Success is a continuing thing.

It is growth and development.

It is achieving one thing and using that as a stepping

stone to achieve something else.

— J O H N   C .   M A X W E L L

Six Habits of Highly *Defective* People

They have a losing attitude. People generally get whatever they expect out of life. Expect the worst, and that's what you'll get.

They quit growing. People are *what* they are, and they are *where* they are because of what has gone into their minds.

They have no game plan for life. As William Feather, author of *The Business of Life,* says, "There are two kinds of failures: Those who thought and never did, and those who did and never thought."

They are unwilling to change. Some people would rather cling to what they hate rather than embrace what might be better because they are afraid of getting something worse.

They fail in relationships with others. People who cannot get along with others will never get ahead in life.

They are not willing to pay the price for success. The road to success is uphill all the way. Anyone who wants to accomplish much must sacrifice much.

The highest

reward for your work

is not what you get for it, but what

you become by it.

— J O H N   C .   M A X W E L L

BIRDS OF A FEATHER

For years, Monterey, California, was a pelican's paradise. The town was the site of many fish canneries. In fact, it was the home of Cannery Row, a street popularized by Nobel Prize-winning author John Steinbeck in his novel of that name.

Pelicans loved the town because fisherman cleaned their catch, discarding the offal, and the pelicans would feast on those scraps. In Monterey, any pelican could be well fed without having to work for a meal.

But as time went by, the fish along the California coast were depleted, and one by one, the canneries all shut down. That's when the pelicans got into trouble. You see, pelicans are naturally great fishers. They fly in groups over the waves of the sea, and when they find fish, they dive into the water and scoop up their catch. But these pelicans hadn't fished in years. They had grown fat and lazy. And now that their easy meals were gone, they were actually starving.

Environmentalists from the area wracked their brains to figure out a way to help the pelicans, and finally they came up with a solution. They imported pelicans from another area, ones that were used to foraging every day, and they mixed them in with the local birds. The newcomers immediately started fishing for their own food, and it wasn't long before the starving native birds joined them and started fishing for themselves again.

If you find yourself starving for success, one of the best ways to get things going in your life is to be around people who are achieving success. Spend time with them. Watch how they work. Learn how they think. You will inevitably become like the people you are around.

It's right to be content with what you have,

but not with what you are.

— AUTHOR UNKNOWN

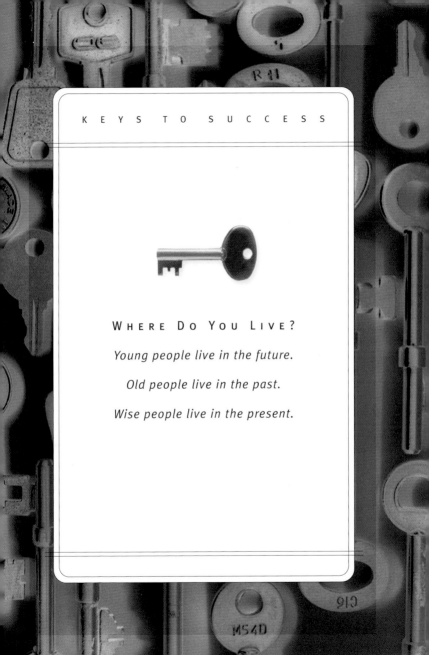

WHERE DO YOU LIVE?

Young people live in the future.

Old people live in the past.

Wise people live in the present.

TIME ON YOUR HANDS

Look at your day. How do you spend it? What ruts have you gotten yourself into that you could easily break yourself out of? What poor habits are eating valuable minutes of your life every day?

What impact can a few minutes make? Take a look at this. What if you were able to save . . .

Five minutes by streamlining your morning routine (taking less time to dress, shave, put on makeup, drink coffee, read the paper, and so on)?

Ten minutes by eliminating the things you do each morning to stall starting your work or school day?

Five minutes by avoiding idle talkers or other distractions?

Ten minutes by taking a shorter lunch or break time?

Those minutes don't seem like much. But if you did those things every day, five days a week, for fifty weeks, you would gain an additional 125 hours of time every year. (That's the equivalent of more than *three forty-hour weeks* to use for anything you want!) And if you're a television watcher, you can *double* the time you gain each year if you simply watch thirty fewer minutes of television every day.

Time is usually wasted

in the same way every day.

— PAUL MEYER

THE TOP TEN HIGH-VALUE
USES OF YOUR TIME

Things that advance your overall life purpose.

Things you have always wanted to do.

Things that others say can't be done.

Things that help you grow to your maximum potential.

Things that develop other people's ability to achieve and lead.

Things that multiply—rather than merely add—
value to yourself and others.

Things that harness your creativity.

Things you can delegate to others.

Things that promote teamwork and synergy.

Things that are *now or never* opportunities.

Success is not perfection;

success is slightly above average.

— ANONYMOUS

Life is like riding in a taxi.

Whether you are going anywhere or not,

the meter keeps ticking.

— JOHN C. MAXWELL

IT'S NOT ABOUT MONEY

Wealth and what it brings is at best fleeting. For example, in 1923, a small group of the world's wealthiest men met at the Edgewater Beach Hotel in Chicago, Illinois. They were a "Who's Who" of wealth and power. At that time, they controlled more money than the total amount contained in the United States Treasury. Here's a list of who was there and what eventually happened to them:

Charles Schwab: president of the largest independent steel company—died broke.

Arthur Cutten: greatest of the wheat speculators—died abroad, insolvent.

Richard Witney: president of the New York Stock Exchange—died just after release from Sing Sing prison.

Albert Fall: member of a U.S. President's cabinet—was pardoned from prison so that he could die at home.

Jess Livermore: greatest "bear" on Wall Street—committed suicide.

Leon Fraser: president of the Bank of International Settlements—committed suicide.

Ivar Kreuger: head of the world's greatest monopoly—committed suicide.

Even Greek millionaire Aristotle Onassis, who retained his wealth and died at a ripe old age, recognized that money isn't the same as success. He said, "After you reach a certain point, money becomes unimportant. What matters is success."

FROM *THE SUCCESS JOURNEY*

Self-trust is the

first secret of success.

— ANONYMOUS

BASEBALL DIARY

Years ago a young baseball player's long-ball hitting got the attention of a pro scout, and the boy was offered a contract. When he went off to spring training, he performed well. And each week he wired his mother back at home in Mississippi to inform her of his progress.

Week One: "Dear Mom, leading all batters. These pitchers aren't so tough."

Week Two: "Dear Mom, looks like I will be starting in infield. Now hitting .500."

Week Three: "Dear Mom, today they started throwing curves. Will be home Friday."

THE SILENT LESSON:
TEACHABLITY

I f you see the image of a little man sporting a tiny moustache, carrying a cane, and wearing baggy pants, big clumsy shoes, and a derby hat, you know immediately that it's Charlie Chaplin. Just about everyone recognizes him. In fact, in the 1910s and 1920s, he was *the* most famous and recognizable person on the planet. If we looked at today's celebrities, the only person even in the same category as him in popularity would be Michael Jordan. And to measure who is the bigger star, we would have to wait another seventy-five years to find out how well everyone remembers Michael.

When Chaplin was born, nobody would have predicted great fame for him. Born into poverty as the son of English music hall performers, he found himself on the street as a small child when his mother was institutionalized. After years in workhouses and orphanages, he began working on the stage to support himself. By age seventeen, he was a veteran performer. In 1914, while in his mid-twenties, he worked for Mack Sennett at Keystone Studios in Hollywood making $150 a week. During that first year in the movie business, he made thirty-five films working as an actor, writer, and director. Everyone recognized his talent immediately, and his popularity grew. A year later, he earned $1,250 a week. Then in 1918, he did something unheard of. He signed the entertainment industry's first $1 million contract. He was rich; he was famous; and he was the most powerful filmmaker in the world—at the ripe old age of twenty-nine.

Chaplin was successful because he had great talent and incredible drive. But those traits were fueled by teachability. He continually strived to grow, learn, and perfect his craft. Even when he was the most popular and highest paid performer *in the world*, he wasn't content with the status quo.

Chaplin explained his desire to improve to an interviewer:

When I am watching one of my pictures presented to an audience, I always pay close attention to what they don't laugh at. If, for example, several audiences do not laugh at a stunt I mean to be funny, I at once begin to tear that trick to pieces and try to discover what was wrong in the idea or in the execution of it. If I hear a slight ripple at something I had not expected to be funny, I ask myself why that particular thing got a laugh.

That desire to grow made him successful economically, and it brought a high level of excellence to everything he did. In those early days, Chaplin's work was hailed as marvelous entertainment. As time went by, he was recognized as a comic genius. Today many of his movies are considered masterpieces, and he is appreciated as one of the greatest filmmakers of all time. Screenwriter and film critic James Agee wrote, "The finest pantomime, the deepest emotion, the richest and most poignant poetry were in Chaplin's work."

If Chaplin had replaced his teachability with arrogant self-satisfaction when he became successful, his name would be right up there along with Ford Sterling or Ben Turpin, stars of silent films who are all but forgotten today. But Chaplin kept growing and learning as an actor, director, and eventually film executive. When he learned from experience that filmmakers were at the mercy of studios and distributors, he started his own organization, United Artists, along with Douglas Fairbanks, Mary Pickford, and D. W. Griffith. The film company is still in business today.

FROM *The 21 Indispensable*
Qualities of a Leader

You don't really pay for things with money.

You pay for them with time.

"In five years, I'll have put enough away

to buy that vacation house we want.

Then I'll slow down."

That means the house will cost you five years—

one-twelfth of your adult life.

Translate the dollar value of the house,

car, or anything else into time,

and then see if it's still worth it. . . .

The phrase spending your time *is not a metaphor.*

It's how life works.

— CHARLES SPEZZANO

A CALL TO ARMS

During World War II, the allied forces called every available man to be ready to fight in the Battle of the Bulge. A unit consisting of clerks and office workers was hastily converted to infantry and assigned to a section of the road that was expected to be under fire within hours.

The men were ordered to dig foxholes from which to fight. One man, who had spent years at a typewriter, tried his best but made little progress in the stone-hard ground. Finally, he approached his lieutenant and said, "Sir, wouldn't it be easier if we just attacked and made *them* dig the foxholes?"

Until you value yourself,

you won't value your time. Until you value your time,

you will not do anything with it.

— M. SCOTT PECK

THE TRUE MEASURE OF SUCCESS

To be able to carry money without spending it;

To be able to bear an injustice without retaliating;

To be able to do one's duty when critical eyes watch;

To be able to keep at a job until it is finished;

*To be able to do the work
and let others receive the recognition;*

To be able to accept criticism without letting it whip you;

To like those who push you down;

To love when hate is all about you;

To follow God when others put detour signs in your path;

*To have a peace of heart and mind because
you have given God your best.*

This is the true measure of success.

— AUTHOR UNKNOWN

FAME ISN'T WORTH A FLEA

Walt Disney was once asked, "How does it feel to be a celebrity?" This was his answer:

"It feels fine when it helps to get a good seat for a football game. But it never helped me to make a good film, or a good shot in a polo game, or command the obedience of my daughter. It doesn't even seem to keep fleas off our dogs—and if being a celebrity won't give one an advantage over a couple of fleas, then I guess there can't be much in being a celebrity after all."

Don't confuse fame with success.

Madonna is one; Helen Keller is the other.

— ERMA BOMBECK

GIVE GOD THE FIRST

Give God the first part of every day.

Give God the first day of every week.

Give God the first portion of your income.

Give God the first consideration in every decision.

Give God the first place in your life.

— JOHN C. MAXWELL

Perhaps it would be a good idea,

fantastic as it sounds, to muffle every telephone,

stop every motor and halt all activity

for an hour some day to give people a chance to

ponder for a few minutes on what it is all about,

why they are living, and what they really want.

— JAMES TRUSLOW ADAMS

THE HOT POKER PRINCIPLE

If you place a poker near the
heat of a fire, it too becomes hot.
To succeed, follow the
hot poker principle.

- *Be around great men and women,*
  and learn from their experience.
  - *Visit great places.*
  - *Attend great events.*
  - *Read great books.*

INSIDE OUT

Most people approach success from the outside in. But to achieve real success, you have to do it from the inside out. Focus on your character, and your whole life improves. Changes in character bring substance and power, while external improvements are merely cosmetic and quickly fade away.

Faced with crisis,

the man of character falls

back on himself.

— CHARLES DE GAULLE

Having potential
works exactly opposite to the way
a savings account does.
In a savings account, as time goes by,
your money compounds interest.
The longer you leave it untouched,
the more it increases.

When it comes to potential,
the longer you leave it untouched,
the more it decreases.
Unused potential wastes away.
If you want your potential to increase,
you have to tap into it.

— J O H N C. M A X W E L L

A STORMY NIGHT

 ate one blustery night, an elderly couple dashed out of the rain and into the lobby of a small Philadelphia hotel, hoping to secure a room for the night. But much to their disappointment, the hotel was full.

"There are three conventions in town," said the cheerful front desk clerk. "I'm afraid all the hotels are full."

The couple started to turn away, and the clerk continued, "But I can't send a nice couple like you out in the rain at one o'clock in the morning. Would you be willing to sleep in my room? It's not exactly a suite," he added, "but it will make you comfortable for the night."

The couple was reluctant to put the man out, but he insisted. "Don't worry about me. I'll make out just fine," he said, and they finally accepted his offer.

When they checked out the next morning, the elderly gentleman said to the clerk, "You are the kind of manager who should be the boss of the best hotel in the United States. Maybe someday I'll build one for you." The man at the desk simply smiled and thanked them.

Two years later, the hotel clerk received a letter from the

elderly gentleman. In it was a round trip ticket to New York City and a note. The note reminded the clerk of the night he had helped the couple and invited him to come up to visit them. Though he had nearly forgotten the incident, he decided to take them up on their offer.

They met him at the station in New York and then took him to the corner of Thirty-fourth Street and Fifth Avenue.

"That," said the elderly man, pointing to a mammoth new building made of reddish stone on the corner, "is a hotel I have just built for you to manage."

"You must be joking," the clerk said.

"I can assure you that I am not," said the old gentleman with a smile. The elderly man's name was William Waldorf Astor. The huge turreted building was the original Waldorf-Astoria Hotel. And the young clerk was George C. Boldt, the hotel's first manager.

An unused life is an early death.

— ANONYMOUS

IF YOU WANT HAPPINESS

If you want happiness for an hour—
take a nap.

If you want happiness for a day—
go fishing.

If you want happiness for a month—
get married.

If you want happiness for a year—
inherit a fortune.

If you want happiness for a lifetime—
help others.

— CHINESE PROVERB

THE RACE AT SUNRISE

Every morning in Africa,

a gazelle wakes up. It knows that it must run

faster than the fastest lion,

or it will be killed.

Every morning a lion wakes up.

It knows that it must outrun the slowest gazelle,

or it will starve to death.

It doesn't matter whether you are a lion

or a gazelle; when the sun comes up,

you had better be running.

— AFRICAN PARABLE

THE TWENTY-FOUR HOUR RULE

Don Shula, former coach of the Miami Dolphins, is the only coach to have led his NFL team to a perfect season and a Super Bowl victory. His secret? When he coached, he held to a twenty-four hour rule. After a football game, he allowed himself, his coaches, and his players only twenty-four hours to celebrate a victory or sulk over a defeat. During that time, they were encouraged to make the most of the experience. But once the twenty-four hours were over, they had to put it behind them.

You don't have to be a football player to benefit from that advice.

There are two types of people

who never achieve much in their lifetime.

The person who won't do what he is told, and the

person who does no more than he is told.

— ANDREW CARNEGIE

The Three "Cs" of Growth

These three words will determine your growth.

CHOICE —it allows you to *start* growing.

CHANGE —it allows you to *keep* growing.

CLIMATE —allows you to *enjoy* growing.

I long to accomplish a great and noble task;

but it is my chief duty and job to accomplish humble

tasks as though they were great and noble.

The world is moved along,

not only by the mighty shoves of its heroes,

but also by the aggregate of the tiny

pushes of each honest worker.

— HELEN KELLER

K E Y S   T O   S U C C E S S

The reward for work

well done is the opportunity

to do more.

— J O N A S   S A L K

STOP, LOOK, AND LISTEN

Stopping to know what you're doing and why isn't a one-time activity. It must be a daily activity. Spend time every morning or evening to think about the coming day. Set aside a day twelve times a year to plan your month. And spend one whole week each year reflecting and evaluating, to measure the year that's passed, to plan the year that's coming, and to stay on track with your purpose.

The world stands aside

to let anyone pass who knows

where he is going.

— DAVID STARR GORDON